MIKE ED

CRAFTS AND TRADITIONS OF THE CANARY ISLANDS

SHIRE ETHNOGRAPHY

Cover photograph
The basketry workshop of D. Juan Ramírez
in Santa Lucía de Tirajana, Gran Canaria.
(Courtesy of the Museo Canario, Las Palmas.)

British Library Cataloguing in Publication Data:
Eddy, Mike.
Crafts and Traditions of the Canary Islands — (Shire ethnography; 17).
1. Canary Islands. Handicrafts.
I. Title.
745'.09649.
ISBN 0-7478-0011-1.

Published by
SHIRE PUBLICATIONS LTD
Cromwell House, Church Street, Princes Risborough,
Aylesbury, Bucks HP17 9AJ, UK.

Series Editor: Bryan Cranstone

ISBN 0 7478 0011 1.

First published 1989.

Printed in Great Britain by
C. I. Thomas and Sons (Haverfordwest) Ltd,
Press Buildings, Merlins Bridge, Haverfordwest, Dyfed.

Contents

Acknowledgements

This brief, introductory sketch of present-day traditional Canary Island life and its roots is the outcome of many years' research, often under difficult political circumstances, by professional colleagues, private individuals and various institutions too numerous to list one by one. However, of all these I must give pride of place to Marcos Hormiga, who first introduced me to Canarian folk music and to *lucha canaria*. I am equally indebted to the Board of Governors of the Museo Canario, in Las Palmas de Gran Canaria; to the museum's ever helpful library staff; and particularly to Don Julio Cuenca, the curator, and his assistant, Don Guillermo Rivero, as well as all those who have contributed to the *Plan Especial de Guayadeque*. I also owe a considerable debt of gratitude to Don Jesús Gómez of Cho' Zacarias, San Mateo, in Gran Canaria, for allowing me access to his comprehensive collections and to his extensive knowledge of Canarian rural life. Finally, I must thank Moira for her encouragement, support and astute criticism during the preparation of the typescript.

Unless otherwise indicated, photographs and figures are by the author.

List of illustrations

1
Introduction

Generalising about the Canary Islands is fraught with difficulties. Each of the seven main islands of the archipelago can be distinguished for a host of geographical and social reasons. All are volcanic in origin, though the vast lava field which enveloped a third of Lanzarote in the eighteenth century is quite different from the huge volcanic cone that forms the 3718 metre (12,200 feet) high Mount Teide on Tenerife.

As the islands are strung out in a rough arc off the coast of North Africa, they enjoy a Mediterranean climate moderated by their oceanic position. The westernmost islands of La Palma and El Hierro are well watered and verdant, whereas the low easterly islands of Fuerteventura and Lanzarote seem more akin to the Sahara. This range of climates from west to east, combined with the effects of altitude, has resulted in a remarkable variety of micro-climates within which plant, and some animal, species have been able to evolve virtually unaffected by the ice ages.

However, the islands are not of note solely for their endemic plants or their classic volcanic geology. They also possess considerable archaeological and ethnographic interest.

Guanche culture

As European sailors pushed south along the African coast and west into the Atlantic during the thirteenth and fourteenth centuries, the precursors of Columbus discovered the Canary Islands, though they were not the first arrivals. The islands had already been occupied by tribal groups which depended in the main on a pastoral economy combined with fishing and limited agriculture. These native islanders lived in artificial or natural cave-houses, though, principally in Gran Canaria and Fuerteventura, the commoners built semi-sunken houses with dry-stone walls.

The tourist literature abounds with references to the 'mystery of the Guanches', the name commonly applied to the pre-Hispanic inhabitants of the islands (though strictly speaking it should only be used for native islanders of Tenerife). The only real 'mystery' surrounding the Guanche culture is the question of when the first settlers arrived and, as more radio-carbon dates become available, this is being clarified. The settlement of Tenerife took place, on present evidence, some time between

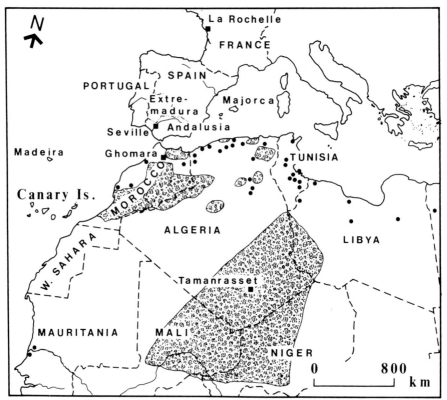

1. Location of the Canary Islands. The areas where Berber languages are still spoken are stippled; important Berber-speaking townships are designated by a black dot. European towns and regions important in the Canarian conquest are also shown.

about 500 BC and AD 1. The immigrants were Berber speakers from adjacent North Africa and many modern place-names can be closely paralleled with place-names there: the island of Gomera with Ghomara in northern Morocco and the hispanicised Tamaraceite, Gran Canaria, with Tamanrasset in Algeria, for example.

Parallels exist in the archaeological record too. Fortified rock-cut granaries exist on both sides of the strait between Cape Juby and the islands. Dry-stone burial cairns and the use of caves by the living and the dead are shared features. The early Berbers in North Africa used fire-hardened spears, as did the native islanders at the time of the conquest. The parallels are legion and are particularly clearly seen in pottery-making and the organisation of the pottery industry (see chapter 2).

European conquest

The European chronicles of the contact and conquest period describe the islanders as white-skinned, blonde-haired and powerfully built. During this time, European merchant adventurers were attracted to the islands as much — or perhaps more — by the prospect of slave-raiding as by trading for orchil (a lichen used in the medieval dye industry), medicinal 'dragon's blood' (the sap of the dragonia tree) and goat skins. The slave trade brought the islands to the attention of the Papal court and some secular lords, and the principate of the 'Fortunate Islands' was claimed on behalf of several European royal houses.

However, it was not until 1402 that a serious invasion of the islands was planned. Jean de Bethencourt, a Norman-French nobleman, mounted an expedition to establish a lordship in the islands and, landing first in Lanzarote, seized not only that island, but also adjacent Fuerteventura, El Hierro and perhaps La Gomera. However, limited supplies and dissension among his mixed French and Spanish fellow-adventurers forced de Bethen-

2. Drawing of a native woman from the island of Gomera, by Leonardo Torriani, end of the sixteenth century. (Museo Canario.)

3. Circular clay *pintadera* or stamp from Gran Canaria, used in the pre-Hispanic period to mark the sealing of a grain storage pit. Harvested grain was stored in both communal defended granaries and household silos. (Museo Canario.)

court to seek the aid of the Spanish Crown in holding on to the islands.

Despite constant pressure and superior armaments, it took Spain until the final decade of the fifteenth century to subdue all the islands. Indeed, when Columbus passed through the archipelago on his first voyage to the Americas, both La Palma and Tenerife were still independent and the last opposition on Gran Canaria had been crushed barely nine years previously. Although the native population was drastically reduced by slaving, infectious diseases, starvation and several spectacular suicides, large numbers of defeated islanders did survive, some intermarrying with the conquerors, others maintaining something of their old life-style in isolated and marginal areas.

Europeanisation and christianisation of the natives were promoted by the Holy Inquisition and by a secular government influenced by the reconquest of Moorish Spain and the 'purity' of Spanish blood. Nevertheless, it took the Spanish Crown some three hundred years to christianise many native festivals and, despite long years of prohibition, it proved impossible to stamp out native sports (see chapter 7). Even in the late nineteenth century the pre-Hispanic rite of burial in caves persisted in Jandía, Fuerteventura.

4. Seventeenth-century reconstruction drawing of a Guanche-culture burial cave, published by O. Dapper in 1668. (Museo Canario.)

New World and British influences

In many ways it was Columbus's discovery of the New World that allowed many pre-Hispanic traditions and crafts to persist, for, rather than the islands being swamped by the Iberian colonists, the archipelago acted mainly as a calling-off point on the way to and from the Americas.

Close contact did develop between the islands and South America, initially through trade and steady migration. Later, in the late nineteenth and early twentieth centuries, through mass migration caused by the collapse of one mono-culture system after another (see chapter 8), these links became even closer. Canarian migrants formed important minorities in Cuba, Venezuela, Colombia and Uruguay, and one group of Lanzaroteños was instrumental in the foundation of San Antonio, Texas. Emigration from the islands has resulted in the exportation of *lucha canaria* (Canarian wrestling) and *gofio* (fine-ground roasted flour) to those countries, and in the importation of Latin-American themes into the Canaries, particularly into their music

5. The bust of Columbus stands in the square named after him in Las Palmas, Gran Canaria. Behind is the colonial-period priory and church of San Francisco.

and festivals. Canarian Spanish remains much closer to South American Spanish than it is to that spoken on the peninsula, and Spanish-speaking America during the Wars of Independence was the breeding ground for the islands' own independence movement.

The fourth influence to be seen in Canary Islands culture has come from northern Europe, and from Britain in particular. As early as the sixteenth century English merchants were buying malmsey wine and selling cloth in the islands. It was not until the closing years of the nineteenth century, however, when British steamship companies established coaling facilities in Las Palmas, Gran Canaria, that the British presence made itself clearly felt. For good or ill, the British have been responsible for the development of the port of Las Palmas; for the first road, sewerage and lighting systems; and for the development of banana and tomato growing. They were also the first tourists. English words, like *móni* (money), *trinqui* (drinkies), *Chóni* (Johnny — foreigner), have been adopted into Canarian Spanish, whilst the mannerisms of Gran Canaria's 'English colony' during the 1920s were recorded in Alonso Quesada's prose works *Banana Warehouse* and *Las Inquietudes del Hall.*

6. The British Club, Las Palmas, Gran Canaria, now an anachronism between modern tower blocks. In its heyday, with the British church in the nearby suburb of Ciudad Jardín (Garden City), it formed the heart of a thriving British business colony.

2
Pottery

Early pottery

Guanche-culture pottery was handmade or in some cases fashioned on a *tournette* or slow-wheel. Forms varied from one island to another, as did the means and styles of decoration. Tenerife, where the native ceramics have been well studied, seems to be broadly representative of the coarse-ware tradition found on all the islands. There, pre-Hispanic pottery vessels are invariably round-bottomed and occasionally decorated with incised lines on and just below the rim. Those of La Palma were similar in shape but often highly decorated with incised lines and simple stabbed or stamped decoration. On Fuerteventura the commonest style is bag-shaped with some incised decoration on the upper part of the body, though the *tofio*, or milking pot, is incised all over, with a flat base and a broad, angular spout. *Tofios* are still made today on both Lanzarote and Fuerteventura.

On Gran Canaria, however, a fine-ware tradition also existed alongside more utilitarian pots. Flat-based, high-waisted jars with lugs or perforated slab handles and shallow bowls were decorated by 'painting' geometric designs on to the body of the pot. The paints used were apparently ochre-based mixtures which, when heated in the kiln, produced zones of different colours. Evidence from the chronicles suggests that these vessels may have been used as water containers in the home and during rain-making rituals.

Although the Spanish conquest broke down the complex of social and religious relationships which allowed Gran Canaria's distinctive pottery to develop, much of the pottery-making tradition survived.

After the Spanish conquest mainly the semi-industrial forms of the pottery industry survived in the Canaries. New forms (like jugs and sugar moulds) and new techniques (like the use of kilns, rather than bonfire firing) were introduced, though native products were never ousted by imported vessels. Some peninsular potters did attempt to establish themselves on the islands, like the unnamed potter from Seville who approached the Tenerife Cabildo (island council) in the early sixteenth century for a loan of 3000 *maravedis* to set up a pottery producing sugar moulds and wine vats. Others came as tilers to join the post-conquest building boom.

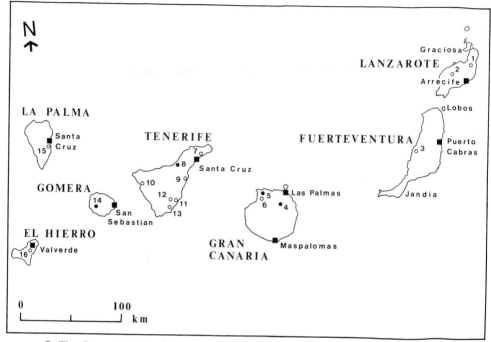

7. The Canary Islands: existing (solid circles) and recently abandoned (open circles) pottery workshops. Main towns are indicated by solid squares. 1, El Mojón; 2, Muñique; 3, Valle de Santa Inés; 4, Atalaya; 5, Hoya de Pineda; 6, Lugarejos; 7, San Andrés; 8, Acentejo; 9, Candelaria; 10, Arguayo; 11, Los Gavilanes; 12, La Cisnera; 13, San Miguel de Abona; 14, Chipude; 15, Santa Cruz; 16, Valverde.

Preparing the clay

However, local producers using traditional sources of material and the established marketing system must have maintained the upper hand. These native potters used friable volcanic soils and ashes, which had to be ground down in mortars to provide suitable potting clay. The resultant clay has the advantages of being easily moulded and firing hard at relatively low temperatures. However, it is also very absorbent in its unfired state and consequently prone to considerable shrinkage.

Once the raw material had been dug out, the potter removed the stones from the soil by hand, sun-dried it and then soaked it in a pit to 'soften' the clay. In Gran Canaria these clay settling pits (*goros*) formed part of the artificial cave complex where the potter worked and lived. The volcanic tuffs from which the caves

8. Pre-Hispanic storage pot with lid, from Gran Canaria. (Museo Canario.)

were cut took up much of the surplus moisture. The potter then puddled the clay with her bare feet and later kneaded it to obtain the right degree of plasticity and smoothness of texture. To increase the clay's plasticity the potter added urine, and volcanic ash was mixed in to improve the adhesive qualities.

Describing the Atalaya, Gran Canaria, potters in 1891, the French anthropologist Lajard wrote: 'The woman — for they are all women who undertake the task — kneels to roll out the clay with her hands. A little sand is spread on the ground to stop it sticking.' The potters at Hoya de Pineda, Gran Canaria, still do the bulk of the preparation and vessel-forming while kneeling or seated on the ground.

Forming the vessels

Most Canarian potters, however, now form their smaller vessels seated at a small table with a stone *tournette* on which the ropes or balls of clay are built up. The vessels are usually made by hand, the larger ones constructed in two halves. After the walls of the vessel have been built up the rim is evened off and the surface

9. Puddling clay at Lugarejos, Gran Canaria. Further inside the cave workshop a batch of platters is drying out on the floor. (Museo Canario.)

10. Forming a pot by hand in an Atalaya workshop, Gran Canaria. (Museo Canario.)

rubbed down with a dampened rag until the fingermarks on the interior and rim have been smoothed out. The wiping helps to mix the sand tempering into the fabric and the thin slurry of clay produced on the pot's surface decreases the vessel's porosity. The skilled potter is able to estimate the smoothness of the surface by the sound made by the rag on the pot. The process is repeated with a piece of felt (often taken from an old hat) until the interior and rim are shiny. It appears that in the pre-Hispanic period pads of grass were used for the same purpose.

The pot is left to dry before the exterior surface is finished off by carving away unwanted clay: implements used are sharpened split canes, a *tijera* (normally part of an old barrel hoop bent over into a U-shaped tool) and *cuchillos* (old domestic knives and again pieces of barrel hoop). Generally Tenerifean potters make thicker-walled vessels which require more carving than do the potters on Gran Canaria. The waste clay is usually mixed into the next load of clay to be worked.

When handles, lugs and spouts are added is dependent on the

potter's preferences. In Gran Canaria such additions are made as the raising of the vessel walls progresses. In Tenerife, however, they are usually added after the surplus clay has been cut away. The vessel is then burnished with a moistened pebble to create a thin top coat of slip or clay wash. In Gran Canaria up to three different stones can be used — the *raspona* (scraper), the *saltona* (smoother) and the *fina* (final polisher).

Decoration techniques

Although in pre-Hispanic times it was a distinctive feature of Gran Canarian pottery, the application of a thin slip of red ochre (commonly, though incorrectly, known as 'paint') is now found on all the islands. Like the clay, the red ochre (*almagre*) is excavated from ancient soils baked by later lava flows (though *almagre* is usually extracted from the upper levels of soil). To raise a shiny surface on the *almagre*-painted areas, the modern potter adds oil and paraffin, though in the not so distant past fish-oil and urine were used. In some cases a slip of the same clay as

11. Finishing off vessels by carving and burnishing at Lugarejos, Gran Canaria. (Museo Canario.)

the main fabric (*engobe*) is applied. Unlike *almagre*, this is done while the vessel is still wet and quite plastic. The only other decoration technique used nowadays consists of light incisions on *bernegales* (water storage vessels) and hanging plates, though reproduction pre-Hispanic pottery from La Palma copies the incised and stamped decoration of the original.

After decoration the pots are given a final burnishing with a smooth pebble. Pebbles with the right qualities for this purpose are highly prized and the potters at Acentejo, Tenerife, use stones that have been handed down over two centuries. In Atalaya, Gran Canaria, the most sought-after stones come from a beach at Arguineguin, over 35 km (22 miles) away in the south of the island.

Firing

The pots are dried indoors in a well ventilated place until they are hard enough to resist the imprint of a fingernail. They are then dried off in the sun in order to remove as much as possible of the remaining water content, especially from the thick bases.

Once a suitable number of vessels has been dried, firing can take place. Although simple down-draught and up-draught kilns

12. Panchito firing the two-hundred-year-old kiln at Atalaya, Gran Canaria, shortly before his death in 1986. (Museo Canario.)

were introduced at the conquest, bonfire kilns were used until recent times on Lanzarote, Fuerteventura, perhaps La Palma and in Lugarejos, Gran Canaria. In Lugarejos the kiln site was a sheltered natural recess in a low cliff. A series of stones placed on edge formed flue channels in which the pots were set and a bonfire was then built over the structure. As far as can be judged, the La Palma kiln was also ground-built, the pots being arranged so as to leave a central flue. In those on Lanzarote and Fuerteventura, however, the vessels were fired over a pit.

Vessel forms

The vessels produced are intimately related to Canarian food processing and cookery. The repertoire includes a number of distinctive forms:

Tostadores or *tiestos* (toasting dishes): flat-based, oval or rectangular dishes used for toasting chestnuts, almonds, coffee, cereals and fern roots, depending on their size.

Braseros (chafing dishes): used for warming food, they comprise three main elements: the stand, rather like a flowerpot with part of the side removed so that charcoal can be put in; a grill forming a top to the vessel; and a rim on which the vessel containing food is placed.

Fogones or *aros*: variants of the chafing dish but with four vertical lugs on which the food container is supported.

Ollas (cooking pots also used for food storage): generally globular or straight-sided vessels, normally provided with four lugs and sometimes with flat, circular lids.

Cazuelas (cooking pots): similar to the *ollas* but with a diameter usually much greater than their height. Used mainly for cooking goat meat.

Bernegales (water storage vessels): squat, wide-bellied vessels in Tenerife; globular and flat-based in Gran Canaria; straight-sided in Lanzarote; and narrow-necked, wide-bodied in Gomera. Sometimes provided with a flat lid on which a cup is kept, they are often incorporated into a *pila*, a wooden frame supporting a stone basin through which water filters into the *bernegal* beneath to provide fresh drinking water (see chapter 5).

Macetas (flowerpots).

Jarretas (large, globular vessels for storing goat's milk): the milk, when allowed to curdle, is used in cheese-making (see chapter 8).

Microceramica (miniatures): miniature versions of the above forms, given as presents for children at Epiphany.

13. (Top left) *Cazuelo pa' vino* (wine bowl) from Atalaya, Gran Canaria; (top right) fish dish from Chipude, Gomera; (centre left) *bernegal* from La Victoria de Acentejo, Tenerife; (centre right) *brasero* from Hoya de Pineda, Gran Canaria; (left) container for *cuajo* (rennet) from Chipude, Gomera.

Sahumerios (incense burners): those from Hoya de Pineda, Gran Canaria, are similar to *braseros* but those from Chipude, Gomera, are small, bipartite pots with holes around the waist.

Bread ovens: large vessels with part of one side cut away and designed to stand mouth-downwards. Some have built-in floors.

Individual potteries

There have been repeated descriptions of the pottery-making

village of Atalaya, Gran Canaria, since the late nineteenth century, probably because it was so easily accessible from the English-owned hotels, like Mr Quiney's or Los Frailes, in Tafira, and because its products were sold in the port of Las Palmas.

The late Francisco Rodríguez, known as Panchito, used a large but simple kiln which was reputedly built in the eighteenth century. The pottery and the fuel were stacked on a raised floor and the fire was maintained by feeding wood through the 1 metre (3 foot) square doorway. There was no chimney, smoke escaping via the doorway. The more sophisticated up-draught kilns were, and are, used in the manufacture of tiles.

As he was the last of the traditional potters, Panchito's cave-house and workshop were studied in some detail by Julio Cuenca during the early 1980s. The arrangement of the cave is shown in figure 14. The clay and sand were stored in two of the artificial caves, where the puddling and mixing of the clay also took place. The forming of the vessels was carried out in the central, open-air patio. The living and kitchen accommodation had been altered to

14. Panchito's cave workshop in Atalaya, Santa Brigida, Gran Canaria. 1, basin for clay; 2, basin for clay trimmings; 3, store for sieved sand; 4, unsieved sand (between 3 and 4 is the clay puddling area); 5, stone slab for working clay; 6, triangular stone slab in floor, where Panchito's mother worked the clay; 7, untreated clay store; 8,9 and 10, former kitchen area; 11, clay modelling table; 12, former dwelling, later display area; 13, dwelling and kitchen; 14, central patio; 15, new toilet; 16, former stable.

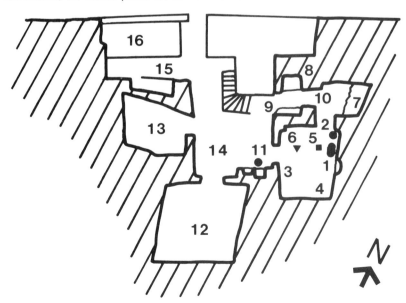

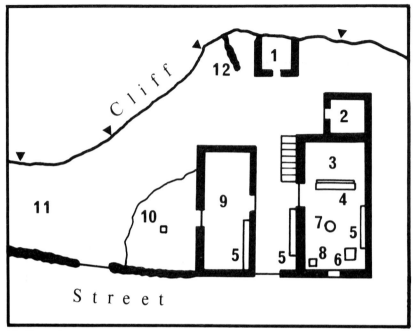

15. Emeteria La Ollera's workshop in Valverde, El Hierro. 1, kiln; 2, cowshed; 3, bedroom; 4, room divider and linen cupboard; 5, work surface; 6, dining table; 7, clay modelling table; 8, sewing machine; 9, kitchen; 10, *aljibe* (water tank); 11, goat-pen; 12, toilet.

make room for a museum-display area and for a bathroom. The old animal pen had become a junk-room. Nevertheless Panchito's cave workshop conforms closely to the Atalaya potter's workshop recorded by Walton in 1957 (though the latter had a circular storage and mixing cave).

The cave workshop can be readily compared with a former potter's house on El Hierro. The island's last potter, Emeteria la Ollera (who inherited her profession from her mother, Antonia), died in 1929, but her house in Valverde survived almost intact for some time. Research by M. Lorenzo Pereta in the late 1970s among the older residents of Valverde allowed a reconstruction of the living arrangements to be drawn (figure 15). The potter lived on the ground floor of the house; upstairs was a separate dwelling. The living quarters were subdivided by a thin partition wall, against which stood a linen cupboard. The bedroom contained only an iron bedstead and the living room housed the sewing machine, the modelling table, the dining table and a 'couple of chairs and a wooden bench'. Puddling the clay was carried out around the *aljibe* (water tank), modelling within the house and firing in a kiln built against a natural rock wall.

A female industry

Despite the reputation of Panchito on Gran Canaria and of Juan Brito on Lanzarote, the traditional pottery industry in the Canaries was dominated by women, as in Berber Africa. Amongst the Berbers the industry takes three principal forms: the purely domestic, the craft household and the semi-industrialised family business. Domestic production is exclusively the province of women, who make vessels for their own use and, by the quality of manufacture and decoration, to enhance their standing in the community. This type of pottery production often involves a certain amount of co-operative effort and, for women in economic difficulty, a means of livelihood as they can supply other households with pots. At Lugarejos, Gran Canaria, the same pattern of mutual aid and interchange of pottery and potting skills for materials and foodstuffs was common into the first half of the twentieth century.

Pottery-making in specialist Berber households is also in the hands of women, though men may be involved in the collection and transportation of fuel and clay. In the Canaries this type of domestic production does not occur, probably because the markets in the post-conquest period favoured a semi-industrial scale of production. Perhaps the only example to be found was in San Miguel de Abona, Tenerife, where pottery-making was in the hands of women whose grandparents had moved from Fuerteventura, bringing with them some techniques normally found only on that island.

The semi-industrial potting villages, like Atalaya on Gran Canaria or Chipude on Gomera, were typical of the Canarian industry. The bulk of the skilled work was carried out by the women, while their menfolk brought in the fuel and clay and more often than not took care of the marketing. In Atalaya at least, men also seem to have been responsible for firing the kilns. In the case of Atalaya, both the clay and the sand tempering came from close by the village, though the *almagre* had to be brought some 15 kilometres (10 miles) over mountain tracks from the centre of the island. The wares were peddled throughout the north-east corner of Gran Canaria.

3
Basketry

One remarkable aspect of the Canarian archaeological heritage is the quality and quantity of organic material that has survived. The cave sites of Gran Canaria, and to a lesser extent Tenerife and La Palma, have produced basketry burial shrouds, matting and containers as well as leather shrouds, bags and even a trouser leg. The stable temperatures and constant humidity levels within the caves created environments in which basketry and leather have desiccated slowly.

Not that the natural process of desiccation adversely affected the suppleness of the leather: at the end of the nineteenth century, the Spanish antiquarian Grau-Bassas reported the use of pre-Hispanic leather by Canarian peasants for making donkey harnesses and shoes. The basketry remains and the cave soils from which they came were used as manure. Those mummified burials not collected by physical anthropologists were dug into the terraced fields.

Nevertheless, much of this material found its way into local and foreign museums: outside Egypt, Canarian basketry probably represents the largest collection of such remains anywhere in Europe or Africa. Regrettably, the European chroniclers paid scant attention to the native basket-makers and their products, generally mentioning them only in passing. Escudero, for example, commented that 'the women weave mats out of beaten and seasoned reeds for blankets and palliasses'. Only when clothing is discussed did the ethnohistorical sources provide useful evidence. Torriani (see figure 2 and figure 37) even illustrated the native costume of some islanders and he wrote of Gran Canaria: 'The Canarians wear fabrics of palm fronds woven together with reeds, with admirable labour and artifice. With these they make various kilts, more or less as do Roman women, and they wrap them around the waist to cover decently their modesty.'

How long native styles of dress survived is unknown, though Torriani must have used first-hand (or good second-hand) evidence as items of clothing like those shown in his drawings have been found on archaeological sites. The need for basketry containers and matting, however, has continued until the present day. The materials used, as well as many of the techniques, are the same now as at the time of the conquest.

16. Raw materials of basket-making: reeds (*junco*) and palm fronds. The reeds in the foreground have been freshly cut. (Barranco de Guayadeque, Gran Canaria.)

The main materials used in earlier times were reeds, rushes and palm fronds and stems. The reeds and rushes grow best near water, so nowadays, because of the excessive extraction of ground watercourses, these materials are in short supply. Today, reeds can normally be found growing only around the leaks in rural water pipes. Deforestation and desertification have seriously reduced the number of palm trees, as they have the stands of cane (*Arundo dorax*, an introduced species) and woodland species used in the heavier basketry.

Reeds

Nevertheless, there are still a number of basket-weavers in Gran Canaria and Tenerife who work with reeds producing clothes baskets (*báules*), *taños* (for storing figs or cheese) and fish traps. The reeds are best cut green, though it is a subject of debate as to whether they can be cut at any time or are best cut in May and June. They are sun-dried and then beaten with a smooth, round stone; the stems are worked wet. Reed can be used together with rush or twisted palm for added strength. In Tenerifean fish traps copper wire is used for tying or stitching the rows of reeds together.

Palm

According to an official survey carried out in 1982, palm is the

17. Border of a pre-Hispanic reed-mat used as the funeral shroud of a mummified burial. (Museo Canario.)

only material used for basketry on all seven islands, despite the reduction in the number of palms. The present distribution of the palm clearly reflects the distribution of artesian wells in the drier eastern islands: of the three centres on Lanzarote two are in the northern, wetter highlands and the third on the isolated islet of La Graciosa. Palm provides a steady supply of materials as the old fronds must be cut away every year to keep the tree in good condition. Regular pruning makes sure that the raw material dries white and stays white when smoked in sulphur.

The palm leaves are used in the making of bags, hats and circular mats, and the stem of the frond (*pírgano*), when split along its length, is used for the principal uprights of the larger or heavy-duty baskets and creels. On the island of La Palma the *pírgano* is also cut into thin strips and woven to produce much finer basketry than is found elsewhere on the islands. *Palanqueta* (thin strips pared from the stalk of a bunch of dates) is used for strengthening the border of the basket.

Osier

In the western islands osier (*mimbre*) baskets are made for storage and heavy-duty work in the fields. Interwoven with other materials, *mimbre* is probably the commonest element in modern Canarian basketry. It is traditionally collected in February and March (preferably when the moon is waning) though Tenerifean basket-makers prefer to cut it in October to avoid damaging the plant.

The cut wands are then stored under cover for a year. In San

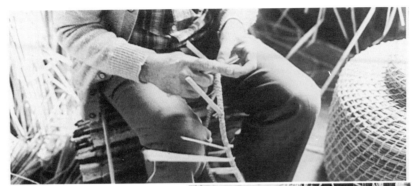

18. Plaiting reed and palm together to make a single strand to be used in producing *taños*. Santa Lucía, Gran Canaria. (Museo Canario.)

19. Finishing off a *taño*, using plaited reed and palm. Santa Lucía, Gran Canaria. (Museo Canario.)

José de los Llanos, Tenerife, the wands are taken out of store as required and buried for between four and six days before they are ready to be worked. Basket-makers in Los Portales, Tenerife, soak the wands in water for two to three weeks so that the bark can be peeled off. In Gran Canaria, the wands are 'planted' vertically in water tanks to keep them supple and make bark-stripping easy. Stripped and unstripped *mimbre* are frequently combined for decorative effect: the stripped wands are creamy white in colour and the unstripped dark brown.

20. (Above left) A clothes basket (baúl) of split cane, made in Valsequillo, Gran Canaria, and displayed in Cho' Zacarias, San Mateo, Gran Canaria. (Above right) A *cesta pedrera* of *pírgano* made in Ingenio, Gran Canaria, and displayed at Cho' Zacarias. It was used for heavy agricultural work, especially clearing stones from cultivated fields. (Below left) A shopping basket of *mimbre* and split cane, made in Valsequillo and provided by Don Francisco Moreno of Tagugüy, Las Palmas, Gran Canaria. (Below right) Two baskets of *mimbre* and split cane, made in Teror, Gran Canaria, and provided by Don Francisco Moreno. In the foreground is a shopping basket; behind is a weeding basket (*cesto pa' hierba*).

Cane and straw

Cane is a popular modern basket-weaving material, though it is rarely used alone. The cane is cut in the winter months and the top of the cane is removed before being stored in the shade to dry.

Rye straw is also used for baskets and hats, though there are differences in the tying or stitching. In Lanzarote the straw is usually tied with reed and in La Palma with longitudinally split bramble.

On La Palma, straw (there known as *colmo*, a word of Portuguese origin, rather than the Spanish *paja*) is woven in a spiral to form a *balaya* (also a word derived from the Portuguese), which is woven from the centre of the base outwards and stitched as the work proceeds. The word *taño* (see page 23) probably also comes from Portuguese. Despite the Portuguese names used in this style of basket-making, the technique may well be pre-conquest in origin: it is found widely in north and west Africa, and Portuguese terms were often adopted for native artefacts and structures.

21. Doña Dorothea Armas, a traditional potter from Muñique, Lanzarote, wearing a hat of woven palm fronds decorated with a strip of ribbon. She is burnishing a tripod pottery vessel. (Museo Canario.)

4
Weaving

The technology of weaving and related textile crafts, as a post-conquest innovation, is no different from that found in peninsular Spain. The loom is a Mediterranean version of the horizontal treadle loom, similar in many respects to the handloom still used by the Hebridean crofter-weavers. Some of the products, however, are unusual.

Traperas

Most tourists visiting the islands will encounter colourful *traperas* in the souvenir shops. A *trapera* (from *trapo*, or rag) is a length of woven material made from thin strips of industrially manufactured cloth. Commercial thread or homespun wool is used for the warp threads, and strips cut from old skirts, dresses and sheets for the weft. The finished fabric is thick and heavy, suitable for rugs, bedspreads or bags, and now often turned into wall-hangings, trunk-covers and even car-seat covers.

Traperas are produced on every island in the archipelago except Lanzarote. An individual length, or *lienzo*, is usually 50 to 65 cm (1 foot 6 inches to 2 feet) wide and can be up to 30 metres (100 feet) long. In Gran Canaria, where looms are generally larger and better made, *lienzos* can be 80 cm (2 feet 4 inches) to 1 metre (3 feet 3 inches) wide.

Decorative designs are restricted to simple, broad bands (*rayas*) of more or less the same colour, or to lozenges (*rombos*) and triangles (*teides*) made up of thinner bands of coloured rags. Normally the *rombos* and *teides* are woven into plain wool *lienzos* to provide greater contrast. The weaving of lozenge and triangular decoration was until recently done almost exclusively by Doña Chira Chinea of Valle Gran Rey, Gomera, though the strongest and the best made *traperas* are generally acknowledged to come from La Palma. Occasionally simple lettering (island or resort names) is woven into bags for sale in the tourist shops. Bedspreads are made by sewing two, three or four lengths of *trapera* together.

Silk

Homespun and woven woollens are still produced on all the islands, but the once flourishing silk industry is now found only on the island of La Palma. Permission to plant mulberry trees on

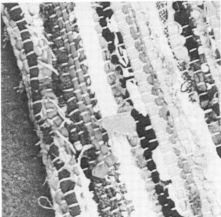

22. (Above) *A trapera* made of 2 metre (3 foot) wide strips joined together and used as a bedspread. (Right) A detail. Provided by Don Francisco Moreno of Tagugüy, Las Palmas, Gran Canaria.

Tenerife was first sought in 1517; Carlos I's warrant of 1538, noting of La Palma that 'in that said isle has begun the making of silk', laid down that the Church was entitled to a tithe of the mulberry leaves, though not of the silk produced on the islands.

Although the silk weavers of Tenerife were producing 'taffetas, black satins and velvets' by the mid sixteenth century, it was not until the early eighteenth century, following the decline in the sugar and wine trades, that the industry became of major importance. The Scottish sea-captain George Glas, writing in

23. (Above) Basket of silkworm cocoons attached to twigs. Each cocoon can provide as much as 450 metres (500 yards) of silk thread. (Left) Silk weaver's loom. (Below left) Hanks of silk thread and silk workers' cane winding frames. (Below) A tailor's dummy showing traditional Canarian costume. The short cape and bodice are of black velvet, the hat is trimmed with black silk and the blouse is of white silk. (At the 1989 La Palma Craft Fair, Mazo, La Palma.)

1764, records the islands of Gomera, Gran Canaria, La Palma and Tenerife as the centres of silk production. In 1735 there were ninety cottage weavers working in Tenerife, eleven of them in Los Realejos; in Orotava, Tenerife, in 1727, there were twenty silk shops, each with two looms, and one with four.

During the first half of the eighteenth century most of the silk was exported to Spanish America. The average produced per loom in Los Realejos, Tenerife, in 1777 was 45 kg (100 pounds). In 1813, when the industry was in decline, total production was 3811 kg (8285 pounds), of which some 2035 kg (4424 pounds) were exported. La Palma was the main producer in the early nineteenth century (2335 kg, 5077 pounds, in 1813), followed by Tenerife (741 kg, 1612 pounds), Gomera (574 kg, 1248 pounds) and Gran Canaria (160 kg, 348 pounds). Palmeran silk workers still use the pound as a unit of measurement.

However, the Canarian silk industry was already in trouble by the end of the eighteenth century, despite the invention of an improved spinning wheel by Agustín de Bethencourt y Molina, an engineer, and his sister, María, a nun and silk weaver in a Tenerife convent. Importation of cheaper English and French cloth, combined with an epidemic among the silkworm population, led to the industry's decline. One late eighteenth-century commentator recorded that silk production was low as many of the 'silkworms died and, despite this, the price of silk has not been high'. The situation was not helped, as the *Sociedad Económica de Amigos del País* pointed out, by the lack of local dye-works. The society recommended a list of natural dyestuffs to the industry and that silk weavers should go the Americas to learn from the Indians how to use them. Instead, the silk industry stagnated behind protectionism and attempts made to revive it when the cochineal industry collapsed in the late nineteenth century did not succeed.

Today in El Paso, La Palma, there is only one spinner and one weaver working, though several women still cultivate silkworms. The worms are bred in caves, known as *moradas*. In the spring the grubs are collected and incubated in the sun by day and under the pillow or between the growers' breasts at night. After forty days the grubs are attached to branches which are placed in boxes containing black mulberry leaves. Here the silkworm creates a cocoon which can provide some 450 metres (500 yards) of silk thread. The larvae are killed in the cocoon by submerging them in a vat of hot water. This is agitated by a small besom and the strands of silk are led on to the spinning wheel. A dozen or more cocoons are needed to produce a single usable silk thread. Assisting the spinner (*hebrera*) are the *sedera*, who maintains the fire and agitates the cocoons, and the *tornero*, normally a man, who turns the wheel and winding frame. The raw silk is washed and bleached and then dyed in the liquid produced by boiling almond shells, one of the methods proposed by the *Sociedad Económica* in the late eighteenth century.

Calados and rosetas

Another facet of the craft textile industry is the production of *calados* (openwork) or, more descriptively, *deshilados* (unthreaded). A *calado* is made by unthreading areas of a linen cloth and working an openwork design in those spaces remaining. The linen is stretched taut within a rectangular frame and then 'marked out' using a needle to remove enough fibres to form the desired design of the openwork. The areas to be removed are then unpicked and sometimes cut out, taking care to secure the loose ends of the fabric. Once the unpicking has been done several craftswomen work together stitching along and between the surviving fibres to produce bands of coarse lace infill within the cloth.

Calados are made in Tenerife, Gran Canaria and Fuerteventura. Table cloths are the commonest product, though handkerchiefs, blouses, dresses, table settings, bedspreads and altar cloths are also produced. Regrettably, much of what is offered to tourists as authentic Canarian *calado* is now made in the Far East: to guarantee authenticity it is best to buy direct from the producer.

On Tenerife and Lanzarote *rosetas* are also made. These are rosettes of coarse lace, sold as doilies or sewn on to table cloths, shawls and traditional dresses and blouses. Women's traditional dresses and blouses are also decorated with embroidery, the costumes and the designs differing from island to island, and even from village to village.

5
Woodworking

The dry and stable atmospheres of Canary Island caves have preserved not only pre-Hispanic leatherwork and basketry (see chapter 3) but also wooden artefacts. Regrettably, however, most of the woodwork found so far has been limited to fire-hardened spears, staves and roughly constructed beds on which to lay out mummified corpses. Only a few rare pieces suggest carpentry of high quality, like the decorated wooden mace and the silo door with handle and pivot-hinge, carved from a single piece of wood, found in the Guayadeque, Gran Canaria.

However, the European chronicles of the conquest and early colonial period reveal otherwise unexpected carpentry skills. Sedeño, writing about 1640, says of native peasant houses in Gran Canaria that 'they roof them with beams and boards of finest *tea* and other hardwoods, which they work with stone blades set in horn, in the manner of adzes'. Later the same author describes the king of Gáldar's dwelling as 'lined all round with *tea* boards, these laid very close and painted over that they seem all of one piece . . .'

Boatbuilding

One aspect of pre-Hispanic Canarian woodworking that was the subject of considerable debate, especially in the Franco years, was the existence (or non-existence) of boat-building skills. No chronicle contemporary with the conquest mentions native boats, and some authors have assumed that the islanders must originally have been exiled to the Canaries by the Carthaginians or Romans. Torriani (see chapter 6) is the only writer to describe Canarian boats. He writes of Gran Canaria: 'They also make boats out of the dragon tree, which they dig out entire, and afterwards they put in a stone anchor, and they navigate with oars and with sails of palm around the coasts of the island; and they had, too, the habit of passing over to Tenerife and Fuerteventura to rob.' This account was written just over a century after the island's conquest and Torriani has been considered to have mistaken a European import for a native product: though why should the islanders have adopted the dug-out canoe when the European vessels they had seen were sea-going barques and their plank-built gigs?

The isolationist thesis also fails to take into account the reference in *Le Canarien* (the fifteenth-century chronicles of de

24. Pre-Hispanic tree-trunk coffin from Agaete, Gran Canaria. Excavated by Don Sebastián Jiménez Sánchez. (Museo Canario.)

Bethencourt's conquest) to a Gomeran slave who was the 'brother' (or more likely a cousin) of the king of El Hierro.

Timber construction

Such evidence as there is in the historical sources implies the existence of skilled woodworkers who used stone tools. Whether native craftsmen were able to capitalise on the massive post-conquest building boom is unknown, but the demands on timber were clearly reflected in the ordinances of the island councils concerned by the reduction of the forests within less than two generations. Modern estimates are that barely 1 per cent of the endemic laurel forest survives on Gran Canaria and on nearby Tenerife the proportion is under 10 per cent. The islands' pine forests have been similarly diminished, though there has been some replanting. The Canarian pine produces two standards of usable timber: *tea* (which is used in building work) and *albura* (whitewood used mainly in joinery or for charcoal).

Traditional woodworking is most evident in timber construction. The timber elements of traditional Canarian architecture are all imported from mainland Spain, though the wooden window frames and shutters, doors and, especially, balconies have developed different insular styles. The Canarian balcony in its simplest form is little more than a box projecting from the house wall. The supporting joists may be covered with planking

25. (Above) Typical Canarian covered balcony with lattice-work panels above solid wood panels up to guard-rail height. Above the rail, the balcony has been infilled almost to roof height by lattice panels. Opening lattice panels have been provided above and below the guard rail. (Icod, Tenerife.) (Right) A wooden *pila*, near Bandama, Gran Canaria. The stone basin set into the top of the stand is now used for growing ferns, but the *bernegal* beneath still remains in place.

or exposed and decorated; the balustrading may be entirely of lattice-work panels, or the lattice-work may be supported by a series of solid panels set into a frame. More developed forms have a simple wooden roof unconnected to the balcony, as in the Casa de Colón in Las Palmas, Gran Canaria. More usually the roof, which may also be tiled, is supported on slender pillars usually surmounted by simple capitals similar to an ox-yoke in shape.

The lattice-work panels of the balustrades are designed to be opened, originally so that the young women of the house could talk to their *novios* (suitors): the balustrades are sometimes up to chest height. In less grand houses, lattice-work or solid wood panels within the shutters served the same purpose. San Sebastián, Gomera, and Los Llanos de Aridane, La Palma, have several fine examples of these shutters within shutters.

The heavy Spanish doors found in the historic centres of the old Canarian towns generally became less ornate over time, though the form remains essentially unchanged. The doors are panelled and double-leafed; the hinges are heavy dowels let into the lintel and threshold. As they are set into thick stone walls, the lintels and thresholds are wide. The sides of the embrasure are also lined with wood, which allows the door to be locked both by a key from the outside and by a movable metal bar, called a *tranca*, fixed to the inside edge of the door frame.

26. Carved wooden *caja* (box) of *tea* (pine wood) from Gran Canaria, displayed at Cho' Zacarias, San Mateo, Gran Canaria. Note the wooden bench and the double-leaf door in the background.

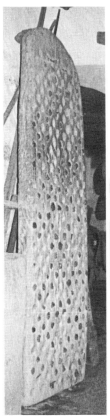

27. (Left) A *trillo* (threshing implement) from Arucas, Gran Canaria. Length: 1.9 metres (6 feet). Displayed at Cho' Zacarias, San Mateo, Gran Canaria.

28. (Below) *Canga* (light yoke) of *alamo* wood from Garafia, La Palma; (bottom) *yugo* (light yoke) of *almo*, from Valsequillo, Gran Canaria. Both yokes are on display in Cho' Zacarias, San Mateo, Gran Canaria.

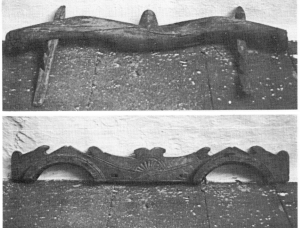

Inside most rural houses and many of the older urban ones is a *destiladera* (on Tenerife and Lanzarote) or a *pila* (on Gran Canaria and La Palma). In its present form this is a wooden or stone stand which supports a porous stone basin and a *bernegal* (see chapter 2). The stone basin allows water to percolate through and drip into the *bernegal* beneath, purifying the water and keeping it cool. This was originally an Arab invention imported into Moorish Spain, from where it reached the Canaries. Examples of the Moorish-style *pila* exist in several houses in La Palma and take the form of a stand fixed to an internal patio wall. The stone basin is at body height on the second-floor level, while the pot is at first-floor level and can be reached through a small door from the gallery. This Moorish type of *pila* is the ancestor of both the modern free-standing *pila* and the balcony.

29. (Above) *Barriletes* (miniature barrels) of mulberry wood made only in El Hierro and used for holding *aguardiente* (literally 'fire water'); (left) wine jug of sabine wood from Gran Ganaria; (below left) *artesa* (large oval open bowl) of sabine wood, from El Hierro, used for mixing bread dough; (below) *gabeta* (communal food bowl) of sabine wood, from El Hierro. A *gabeta* containing the family's meal was originally placed in the centre of the table for everyone to eat from. (All displayed at Cho' Zacarias, San Mateo, Gran Canaria.)

Furniture, tools and utensils

Canarian furniture varies radically in quality. Upper-class houses were well provided with typical Spanish craft furniture, now all but replaced by mass-produced items, while the peasant houses, as in the case of the El Hierro potter (see chapter 2), contained the barest of essentials. Perhaps the most interesting of the furniture pieces are the wooden chests with their carved decoration and rudimentary legs. They are presumably of mainland Spanish origin but, as yet, their history has not been studied.

Other wooden items found within the traditional Canarian home are *queseras*, *morteras* and *loceros*. The *quesera* is a wooden base, usually supported on three legs, for forming cheeses (figure 50). The board is circular, oval or rectangular in shape with a projection from one side. On the main part of the board a shallow circular channel is cut, with the area enclosed by the channel cross-cut to prevent the cheese sticking and to provide an identifying mark. The circular channel is linked to another which runs the length of the projecting part of the board.

30. Range of wooden and basketry farm tools in the museum at Betancuria, Fuerteventura. In the centre is a pannier frame for a mule, and on the floor a double-bladed saw and an ard plough. (Museo Canario.)

This serves as an overflow for the whey. *Morteras* are used for grinding down herbs and pottery is displayed on a *locero*. Wooden vessels are also made for the kitchen.

Wood forms an important element in many traditional agricultural tools. The ard plough, now tipped with iron, can occasionally be seen in the Canaries, and in the sandy areas of Lanzarote and Fuerteventura a simple board drawn by a camel is used to turn over the soil. Yokes for ox-ploughs and ox-carts and the carts themselves were, until recently, an important part of the woodworkers' craft, as was the *trillo*, a heavy horse-drawn block of wood set with sharp stones and used in threshing.

Specialist woodworkers manufacturing musical instruments have witnessed a steady growth in the market for their wares as interest in Canarian folk music has revived (see chapter 6). Because of the cost of imported furniture and the increase in building work due to the growth of tourism, woodworking generally has been able to hold its own. Some craft workers, however, have turned to making reproductions in miniature of balconies and *pilas* for the tourist market. Others, making household utensils like *barriletes* (miniature barrels) and *gabetas* (communal food bowls), which no longer serve a purpose, are in a similar position to the last traditional potters (see chapter 2).

31. Miniature balcony made for the tourist trade. (Displayed by Don Francisco Moreno of Tagugüy, Las Palmas, Gran Canaria.)

6
Music and dance

Early music

In the late sixteenth century an Italian engineer, Leonardo Torriani, was contracted by the Spanish Crown to carry out a survey of the military defences of the Canaries, which were then being threatened by the Barbary pirates and English and Dutch raiders. During his stay on the islands he was able to travel widely and he used the opportunity to report not only on the defensive potential of the terrain but also to record the islands' history and customs. As a trained observer, he has left one of the most reliable and objective descriptions of island life. Unlike the earlier chroniclers of the conquest, he was able to make detailed notes on the surviving island society.

Writing of Gomera, Torriani says: 'They sang verses of lamentation, of eight, nine and ten syllables, and with so much sadness that they themselves wept, as those who are descended from the last inhabitants can be seen to do...[the verses'] name is *endechas*, that is, female laments. It is true that they are sung in the other islands, on the occasion of the death of some worthy person, or some sad event; but those of this island are the most beautiful and heart-rending.' He then quotes two examples, one of which is:

> *Aicà maragà, aititù aguahae*
> *Maicà guere, demacihani*
> *Neigà haruuiti alemalai;*

which translates as:

> Welcome thirst, they killed our mother,
> These people from afar, but now together,
> Brother, I would settle down now all is lost.

None of the early chroniclers mentions musical instruments, apart from a type of rattle, and they limit themselves to references to singing, clapping and stamping. The poet Viana, however, writing in 1604, mentions cane flutes, tambours and bagpipes with a wheat-straw reed in the chanter.

Some authors conclude from this lack of chronicle evidence that there was little instrumentation and little musical repertoire beyond ritual chanting. The *endecha* is even considered to be an importation from Europe because of its similarity to Spanish-Jewish laments. The Italian composers quoted by Torriani as having taken up the Canarian *endecha* were writing when the

32. Folk group performing during the festivities to mark the *Rama* in Guía, Gran Canaria.

Jewish *endecha* was already firmly established. The instruments mentioned by Viana have been interpreted simply as typical examples of late medieval peasant instrumentation.

Dance

Whatever may be the case, the Canary Islanders did export one of the earliest dance crazes to hit Europe: the Canarian, the steps of which were published in France in 1588 by Thoinot Arbeau. It consisted of two dancers alternately approaching and retreating from their partner, the steps comprising a series of toe and heel taps followed by a high kicking jump, which was considered in its day to be 'greatly difficult'. Thoinot Arbeau described the dance as 'lively, strange and fantastical, being in great way like unto the dance of the savages'. By the eighteenth century the Canarian had been turned into a courtly and pompous *jota* instead of a truly wild jig. The dance was also exported to South America, initially in its aristocratic form, before entering the popular repertoire there, where it gave rise to the *zapateado* and the *tarantela*.

The Canarian is directly comparable to the present-day *sirinoque* of La Palma and has much in common with the *tajaraste* of Tenerife and Gomera. The word *tajaraste* is Berber in origin and is used of a rattle or tambourine accompanying a dance or chanting. The lyrics sung to accompany the modern Canary Islands *tajaraste* are clearly pagan in origin, despite the use of Mary and Joseph as the two protagonists, and explicit in their reference to fertility, or lack of it:

> *No lo 'jago' mal, Cha'Mariya*
> *Porque yo no tengo con qué:*
> *Que es fisquito pan que tenía*
> *Me lo ruyó un perinquén;*

which translates as:

> It's not that I do it badly, Mistress Mary,
> It's that I don't have the wherewithal,
> 'Cos the titchy little breadstick I once had
> Got nibbled away by a gecko.

By the eighteenth century a number of Iberian traits were beginning to enter the Canarian music repertoire. These became the *folías*, the *malagueñas*, the various *seguidillas* and the *isas*, which form the core of Canarian folk music.

The *folía* was a Spanish courtly dance known throughout Europe by the end of the sixteenth century, and probably introduced into the Canary Islands by the early colonists, though it took over a century to establish itself as a folk dance. In the Canaries, the present-day *folía* preserves the formality of the sixteenth-century original, retaining the traditional element whereby the woman swaps partners but eventually returns to her original partner. The *malagueña*, however, arrived somewhat later, replacing the *fandango* only during the nineteenth century as the favourite dance of the peasantry.

Given the suggestion that the *malagueña* (the Malaga dance) should be renamed the *tinerfeña* (the Tenerifean), the dance and its music have been, and remain, highly popular in the Canaries. Olivia Stone, writing at the end of the nineteenth century, recalls the music for the *malagueña* as 'an inseparable companion during our excursions on horseback or by sea'.

In the eastern islands (Lanzarote, Fuerteventura and Gran Canaria) the *seguidillas* take on their most lively and colourful form, giving rise to the term *seguidillas corridas* (running rhythms).

Another form is known as a *saltona* (leap) because the two singers, who sing alternate verses, repeat the final words of their partners. As a dance, one of the better known *seguidillas* is the *baile de la cunita* (the cradle dance), which is, as the name suggests, a Christmas dance. Performed in Guía, Gran Canaria,

33. (Above) A group of friends making music during the procession of the *Rama* in Guía, Gran Canaria. (Below) A boy blowing a conch shell leads one of the decorated carts down the steep hill from the church during the *Rama* in Guía, Gran Canaria.

it is danced around a full-sized wooden cradle, the men dancing in the opposite direction to the women, so changing partners constantly.

All these dances and tunes are lively and carefree, but the most light-hearted of them all is the *isa*, a term derived from an Asturian (North Spanish) dialect word meaning 'leap'. The *isa* is essentially a local variation of the peninsular *jota* (a word also derived from the verb *saltar*, to leap or jump). In its late nineteenth-century form the *isa* was a lively, individualistic dance, accompanied by castanets, and requiring skilled footwork. Nowadays it has evolved into a variety of different forms, comparable to square dances.

The nineteenth century saw the introduction of a number of Central European dances like the *polca* and *mazurca*. The *berlina* also occurs throughout the archipelago but is only commonly found in Fuerteventura, La Palma and El Hierro.

Musical instruments

The apparently limited pre-conquest instrumentation has been reviewed above. Even Viana, who is the most generous chronicler, is quite certain that stringed instruments were unknown until the Spanish conquest.

Amongst the earliest cases brought before the Inquisition was that of a drunk who played his guitar and sang irreverent verses in a religious procession. Later Inquisition documents and private inventories contain occasional references to guitars and to 'large and small stringed instruments'.

34. Don Francisco Moreno displays a *timple* from Telde, Gran Canaria, made by Don Antonio Súarez Mejías using four different woods.

35. Tambour (drum) from Gomera, made of chestnut wood and kidskin, demonstrated by Don Francisco Moreno of Las Palmas, Gran Canaria.

The small stringed instrument referred to is almost certainly the *timple*, which to the uninitiated looks like a five-string toy guitar. In the hands of an adult the instrument appears absurd — until it is played. Then one appreciates the musical skill and suppleness of wrist required to play it.

The *timple* is considered to be a Canarian development of the small guitars found in the traditional instrumentation of the Iberian peninsula. According to a tradition recorded by a Lanzarote *timple* maker, the first true *timple* was made in the Las Palmas workshop of a Catalan carpenter called Alpañe at the end of the eighteenth century. Nevertheless, an instrument known as a *tiple* was in existence when a self-instruction book for the guitar was published in Madrid in 1752. *Tiple* was the name used in nineteenth-century Gran Canaria for the modern *timple* and the same term is still used in South America to describe the locally made *timple*. Lothar Siemens, the foremost authority on Canarian music, has suggested an Italian origin in the *chitarra batente* of Calabria, introduced to the Canaries when Italy formed part of the Spanish empire. He does not rule out an African origin, however, such as the instrument being introduced in the sixteenth century to the eastern islands by North African slaves.

The other stringed instruments of the Canaries are found throughout peninsular Spain: the guitar, the lute and the mandolin. Castanets are also used, though locally made forms are extremely heavy. Highly polished goat legbones descending in size and suspended around the neck are used as a small xylophone. The tambour, the *pito* (a cane flageolet) and an Argentinian drum comprise the rest of the instrumentation.

36. Canarian castanets carved out of chestnut wood, from Gomera, demonstrated by Don Francisco Moreno, Las Palmas, Gran Canaria.

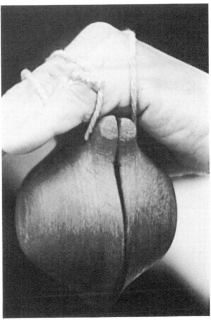

Modern development

Since the death of Franco, Canarian folk music and dance have regained something of their dynamism and social content, and much of the romanticised patriotism laid on for tourists has been forgotten. Important in the resurgence of Canarian folk music have been choral groups like Los Sabadeños, Los Gofiones and Los Granjeros, and the singer-songwriters associated with them. Although traditional songs form a considerable part of the Canarian repertoire, new material using folk music themes has adopted a more political standpoint. This is still a long way from 'protest music', though Canarian separatist sentiments are beginning to find expression.

While Latin American, and particularly Cuban, rhythms have been entering the Canarian repertoire over the past hundred years, Canarian folk musicians have now begun to blend traditional themes with rock music. Taburiente has been particularly influential in this field. One striking aspect for the outsider is the popularity of folk music among the young: the majority of members of the countless *agrupaciones folklóricas* throughout the islands are in their late teens and several groups are based in schools.

7
Sports and festivals

Sports

By far the most popular, and thriving, native sport is *lucha canaria* (Canarian wrestling). Only football and basket ball attract more spectators and wrestling clubs exist on all the islands: there are, for example, fifteen such clubs on Fuerteventura, which has a population of under twenty thousand inhabitants. *Lucha canaria*'s governing body proposed, unsuccessfully, that the sport be included at the 1992 Olympics in Barcelona, as Canarian emigrants have taken it to South and Central America as well as to mainland Spain. Although certainly a native Canarian development, *lucha* is very similar to styles of wrestling found in northern Spain, Switzerland, Celtic Britain and parts of Africa.

The poet Viana describes a late pre-conquest wrestling match in such detail that it is possible to identify all three throws that the winner employs. The prose chroniclers also recorded individual bouts between famous pre-conquest heroes, such as that between Adargoma of Gáldar and Gariragua representing Telde, who met to determine the grazing rights of the kingdoms of Gran Canaria. The known pre-conquest bouts generally took the form of personal duels or trials by combat, though wrestling was also clearly used as a form of training for war or as entertainment at festivities. The native Canarians 'had public places outside the villages, where they held their duels, a circle enclosed by a wall of stone, and a place made high where they might be seen', according to Abreu Galindo, writing in 1602.

In its modern form *lucha canaria* is a team sport, each team comprising twelve wrestlers, only one from each team fighting at any one time. The individual bouts, *bregas*, are fought within a sand-covered ring some 9 to 10 metres (30 to 33 feet) in diameter (the *terrero*, a word of Portuguese origin, perhaps stemming from the temporary alliances between the islanders and the Portuguese against the Spanish). At the start of a *brega* the wrestler takes his opponent's right hand in his and grasps the rolled hem of the opponent's shorts with his left. As they come together their right hands brush the surface of the sand and the *brega* is under way. Using a combination of weight, trips and lifts each man tries to unbalance his opponent. The bout is determined by any part of the wrestler's body, except his feet, touching the ground. Team

37. Pre-Hispanic martial arts, depicted by Torriani. In the left hand the warrior holds a *magodo* or stave, and in the right a throwing stone. (Museo Canario.)

members must win the best of three *bregas* to score a point for their side.

Wrestling retained many of its early characteristics until the Spanish Civil War. Regional variants, similar in style to Cumbrian wrestling, and the presence of a *comisionado* (the wrestler's second) still survived. Even the use of the term 'North' and 'South' in Gran Canaria to denote the two opposing teams reflected the former division of the island into two kingdoms. The folk nature of *lucha canaria* in the early part of the twentieth century is revealed by comments of one Tenerifean writing in 1927: 'Whenever we got together on the threshing-floor, we'd lark around for a bit and then we'd get around to wrestling; and it was quite something to see those lads, big chaps but supple with it, bending like willow, brought down by trips, sidesteps and throws.'

A less widespread, but still practised, sport is *juego del palo*, or stick fighting, which is described in its original form by Torriani, writing in the late sixteenth century: 'When two Canarians challenged each other to a duel, they went to the place agreed upon, which was a raised arena, at each end of which was a flat stone, big enough for a man to stand upright on. First each of

38. (Left) Canarian wrestling (*lucha canaria*): the start of a *brega* or bout. Wrestling teams are sponsored by local businesses.

39. (Right) *Cango por fuera* (a throw in Canarian wrestling): the wrestler facing the camera has hooked his leg behind his opponent's knee to unbalance him.

40. Starting position for a stick fight. Guayadeque, Gran Canaria.

them stood upon the stone, with three stones in his hand, for throwing, and with three more which served for wounding, and with the stave called *magodo* or *amodeghe*. First they threw the stones, which they dodged with skill, weaving their bodies without moving their feet. After, they stepped down to the ground and faced each other with the *magodos*, flourishing them and seeking each his advantage, as is the custom amongst ourselves; and in their fury, managing to smash the other's arm, they wounded him with three thin stones, which they held between the fingers of their left hand.'

The stone throwing and the stone 'knuckle-dusters' are no longer used but the stick-fighting part of such duels survives as a sport or pastime, particularly in areas where goat herding is still common. The staff used is usually about 2 metres (6 feet) long and 3 cm (just over an inch) thick and is made from almost any suitable wood. A pole of the appropriate length is cut green, stripped of its bark, left to season and later cured with pig fat to provide a fighting staff. In Gran Canaria the stick is referred to as a *garrote*, in Tenerife as a *banot* and in Fuerteventura as a *lata*.

There are two main styles of *juego del palo*: the defensive Fuerteventura school, in which power is preferred to speed, and the attacking Tenerife school which sacrifices power for speed.

Like wrestling this was a rural sport up to the time of the Civil War, though it was restricted to goatherds, probably through the early Spanish prohibition of native islanders carrying weapons, from which herdsmen were exempt on the grounds that they needed a suitable stick to defend their flocks. In living memory Fuerteventuran herders met occasionally in a 'Corral Council' to resolve disputes between individual herders and, if agreement could not be reached, the matter was determined by a stick fight.

Occasionally a camel-driver's stick of just under a metre (3 feet) is used. This form of *juego del palo* developed in nineteenth-century Fuerteventura, when camels were first introduced into the islands as beasts of burden or for ploughing. In 1860 the *palo camellero* was imported to Tenerife by Pedro Pestano, and by the 1920s there was a flourishing school on that island. However, this style has all but died out throughout the archipelago.

Unlike other Spaniards, Canarians have no love of bullfighting. The bullrings on Gran Canaria and Tenerife were built before the Franco era to give foreign tourists a taste of the 'real Spain' as seen from Madrid. Gran Canaria's bullring is now derelict and Tenerife's, in the capital Santa Cruz, is no longer used for bullfights, though it remains in use as a stadium for pop concerts and Carnival celebrations. Most Canarians regard bullfighting as a 'barbaric' peninsular custom, though this revulsion does not extend to cockfighting (*peleas de gallo*), a sport which was also introduced from mainland Spain to the Canaries and to South America. In addition, the *bardino*, a heavily built dog with an unusual striped coat, was originally bred as a hunting dog and later developed as a fighting dog by crossbreeding with bulldogs and mastiffs imported by British merchants. Dogfights are now banned though cockfighting remains a legal minority sport.

Festivals

Apart from the major Christian festivals, each village and hamlet has its own fiestas throughout the year and during February the main towns celebrate two weeks of Carnival (though not at exactly the same time). Despite the dominance of the Marian cult in the islands several festivals betray pre-Hispanic origins.

The Matritense chronicle of 1526, for example, gives the following account of a pre-Hispanic rain-making ceremony on Gran Canaria: 'These *Guanartemes* (kings) had each one a *faycan*, who was like to a priest, a man of good example who, in times of scarcity, gathered the people together and led them as in a procession to the sea-shore, with branches and boughs in their

41. Two members of ASPAC, the Canarian Stick-fighting Association, in action.

42. A winning hit to the side of the neck. Both stick-fighters wear traditional shepherds' clothing — linen shirt and short, baggy trousers with a woollen tie belt, woollen leggings and pigskin shoes.

43. An Egyptian theme for the float bearing the Las Palmas Carnival Queen's Lady of Honour, who wears a *fantasia* with an elaborate peacock-fan head-dress.

hands, calling aloud, and they beat on the water with the branches.' Later chronicles add that the processions were accompanied by music and dancing, and that the greenery was collected in the mountains while the *faycan* made offerings of milk and other foodstuffs to the god, Acoran.

A similar custom is still repeated early every August in the village of Agaete, Gran Canaria. Local people and other Canarians parade through the village waving branches, singing and dancing. Though it now takes the form of a popular festival in celebration of the local patron saint, Our Lady of the Snows, and is limited to the village area, Agaete's festival of *La Rama* (The Branch) is clearly a 'Guanche' survival. Older residents of the village recall that well into the twentieth century the local people went into the mountains to cut branches, with which they descended to the sea-shore to beat the surface of the sea. This was accompanied in earlier times by the throb of the tambour, replaced in the 1950s by the music of the town band. Shortly before Agaete's *Rama*, the people of the Valle de Agaete celebrate their *Rama*, which starts in the pine forest of Tamadaba some 1400 metres (4590 feet) above sea level. The descent begins in the early morning, passing the pre-Hispanic cave village of

Berbique, to the outskirts of the town, where the participants are met by Agaete's town band.

A similar fiesta takes place in the neighbouring village of Guía. In its present form it commemorates the salvation of the township's crops from a plague of locusts which occurred around the end of the eighteenth century. However, the story of its origin strongly suggests the survival of similar pre-Hispanic beliefs. According to the tradition, the people of Guía, fearing the total destruction of their crops, gathered on Mount Vergara to collect branches and fruits. They then descended again in procession, singing and praying, in this instance to the Virgin Mary. Though the deities had changed over three hundred years the result was the same, for, so the story goes, a wind sprang up in the west bringing rain, which cleared both the locusts and the hot Saharan air that brought them.

Some authors have sought a late eighteenth-century, peninsular Spanish origin for both these fiestas, but close examination of the available evidence suggests rather that the late eighteenth century was when the Spanish authorities finally imposed their desired degree of Christianity and 'Spanishness' on existing customs.

The towns of Gáldar and San Nicolás de Tolentino, also on Gran Canaria, are equally well known for their *Ramas*, while a similar festival, the *Bajada del Macho* (Descent of the Billy-goat) is celebrated in Ingenio on the same island. In this case the farmers of the area 'elect' the finest of their billy-goats to lead the festive procession into town.

Elsewhere in the archipelago the veneer of Christianity has been more thickly applied and such festivals are known as *bajadas de la Virgen*. The main characteristic is the removal of the Virgin from her usual shrine to a distant town, usually the island capital, where she stays for a period of one month. The *bajadas* of the patron saints of Tenerife (Our Lady of Candelaria) and Gran Canaria (Our Lady of the Pine) are celebrated irregularly. On Gomera (Our Lady of Guadelupe) and La Palma (Our Lady of the Snows) the *bajadas* take place every five years. On El Hierro, the statue of Our Lady of the Magi is taken every four years from its usual residence in the west of the island to the island capital, Valverde, a distance of 40 km (25 miles).

The history of the El Hierro Virgin reveals strong undercurrents of non-Christian belief in the post-conquest period. When the figure of the Virgin was first brought to the island in 1546, it was placed in a cave and in 1577 a sanctuary was eventually built nearby in the valley. Two of the earliest recorded *bajadas*, in 1614 and 1740, were undertaken to counteract the effects of drought and, in 1643, the *Cabildo* (island council) declared the Virgin the 'patron of the waters which are so much lacking in this island, and of the locust'. Originally the Virgin was carried by local shepherds and their elected representatives but in 1944 a *cofradía* or guild was created, comprising the Civil Governor and other notables, to transport the statue.

Carnival, unlike the *Ramas* and *bajadas*, is a winter festival, supposedly pre-Lenten, but able to be moved to any time between Epiphany and Easter: the whole spirit of Carnival is after all a collective nose-thumbing to the established order. The two weeks of chaos and merry-making are presided over by the Carnival Queen, who is elected not on the basis of her looks and personality but rather for the spectacular qualities of her dress. With good reason these creations are known as *fantasías*. For two weeks at a time the islanders dedicate themselves to a series of *verbenas* (which can be loosely translated as 'all-night street parties'). The Carnival parade is a massive affair in which individual creativity is expressed through costume, and popular sentiment is revealed by the lyrics of the *murgas*. These are 'musical' bands whose members dress up in outrageous uniforms and play elaborate instruments made of drainpipes and kazoos.

The final act of Carnival is the Funeral of the Sardine, the King of Carnival. The cortège retraces the Carnival procession route, to the accompaniment of the wailing of the 'widows', mainly men more or less dressed in widows' weeds. Carnival finally ends with the burning of the Sardine on the beach.

Of all the island carnivals, that held in Santa Cruz de Tenerife is without doubt the biggest and the best and was uninterrupted by the Franco dictatorship.

The traditional Christian festivals are celebrated too but are little different from their peninsular counterparts. For the visitor, perhaps the most interesting and visible aspects are the Procession of the Magi at Epiphany and the 'flower carpets' decorating the streets at Corpus Christi.

8
Food and wine

Gofio

Of all the foodstuffs eaten in the Canary Islands today the most typically Canarian is *gofio*. The early sixteenth-century Matritense chronicle mentions it by name, describing it as 'toasted barley flour, which they mill by hand in small querns, and this flour they mix with water or lard or milk, as they mix it today in all the islands and this was their bread'. This was not only so in the sixteenth century: it remains true today, despite the cosmopolitan products on sale in the supermarkets of Las Palmas and Puerto Cruz.

Nowadays, however, *gofio* is rarely milled from barley — maize and millet are used instead — though it is still produced in the few surviving family-owned local mills as well as in fully industrial units.

A glass of milk with *gofio* stirred in is a popular breakfast for many Canary Island families. *Gofio* is also sprinkled into coffee and the congealed lumps swallowed with obvious pleasure. In restaurants *gofio* is normally served as a side dish, either in its raw state as powder or *amasado* (mixed) with milk, oil or stock. Raw *gofio* can be added to *potaje* (usually a vegetable soup), other soups and stews. *Gofio amasado* is simply dipped into, like any other *tapa* (snack), or spoonfuls can be soaked in a soup or stew. Traditionally, *gofio* is mixed in a *zurrón*, a leather bag fashioned out of a whole kidskin. The foreleg and neck openings are plugged and bound up, as are the genitals, and the rear legs are turned into a carrying strap. The *zurrón*, containing *gofio* and either milk or oil, is squeezed and kneaded until the contents have been thoroughly mixed to a dough-like consistency.

European influences

Escudero, writing in the first half of the seventeenth century, listed the foods eaten by the native islanders before the arrival of the Europeans. *Gofio* was 'their staple' and *caldo* (broth, of fish or meat) and 'half-roast, half-raw meat, parboiled if it were thick cut so as to savour the fat and grease' were also important elements in the native diet. In the main meat meant goat meat, though pork was also eaten, and perhaps mutton, although the chronicle sources do not agree on this last point). Goat meat, usually stewed, still maintains its popularity in traditional dishes.

In his list Escudero also recorded the important role played by wild honey, wild fruits like *mocán* berries, shellfish, root crops and 'bitter figs such as there are not in Spain'. Some early chroniclers maintained that figs were introduced only in the fourteenth century, by shipwrecked Majorcan sailors, though Escudero's comment would suggest otherwise. After the European conquest of the islands, however, many new animal and plant species were introduced, as well as improved breeds. Pigs imported from mainland Spain were crossed with the Canarian striped pig to increase its body weight. European goats were

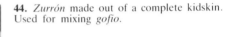

44. *Zurrón* made out of a complete kidskin. Used for mixing *gofio*.

45. The native Canarian goat. The only surviving examples live on small islands off Madeira, though it is planned to reintroduce them to the Canaries. This stuffed specimen is in the store of the Museo Canario, Las Palmas.

46. Beehive made from a hollowed-out palm trunk. This form of beehive is almost certainly pre-European in origin. Guayadeque, Gran Canaria.

introduced and island goats were exported to Madeira and the adjacent islands (often with enslaved Canarian goatherds). Completely interbred with imported goats, the native Canarian goat no longer exists as such in the Canary Islands, though its descendants do still survive on the Desiertas Islands off Madeira. The Canarian striped pig, however, can still be seen in farms throughout the archipelago.

Cattle (which have replaced goats as the mainstay of Canary Island pastoral farming in the larger islands), horses, mules and chickens are all post-conquest introductions, as are crops like sugar-cane, the vine, potatoes and the well known Canary Island tomatoes. These, and the banana, formed the basis of a series of monocultural systems, all of which have contributed to the modern Canary Islander's diet. Sugar-cane, which was introduced to Gran Canaria, Tenerife and the western islands shortly after the conquest, has resulted in the development (aided by mainland Spanish tastes) of a range of extremely sweet (not to say sickly) cakes and desserts, as well as rum. Some of the liqueurs produced in the islands are extremely sweet, like the sticky *ron miel* (honeyed rum) and those based on bananas, coffee and oranges. *Miel de caña* (literally 'cane honey' or molasses) and *bienmesabe* (literally 'know me well', a syrup of honey and almonds) are often poured over ice-cream or yoghurt for dessert.

The sugar industry, however, declined almost as soon as it was established, competition from the large Caribbean plantations proving too much for the small-scale island sugar growers. The grapevine quickly replaced sugar as the main crop and, as it could be grown on all the islands, it formed the mainstay of Canarian agriculture throughout the seventeenth century and has remained important despite outside competition and the demands of other monoculture crops.

By the late sixteenth century, when Thomas Nichols, a Gloucestershire merchant, was trading in the islands, the banana was well established as a food crop. Sixteenth-century tastes were clearly different from modern ones: Nichols comments that the fruit when black 'is finer than any preserve'. The commercial exploitation of the banana on a large scale became possible only in the early years of the twentieth century, when Fyffes and Leacock, among others, set up extensive plantations in the northern districts of Gran Canaria and Tenerife. At the same time early potatoes and early tomatoes also became important cash crops, the former in the well watered foothills of the larger islands and the latter in the sunny coastal plains. Like bananas, these were earlier introductions which had made generally uninspired contributions to Canarian cuisine, with the exception, perhaps, of *papas arrugadas*.

For this dish, *papas* (the islanders use the South American word rather than the peninsular Spanish word for potatoes, *patatas*) are boiled in their skins in a pot of highly salted water. The water is allowed to boil away and the *papas* are then served with a spicy sauce known as *mojo*. This sauce, of hot peppers, oil, garlic and saffron, comes in two forms — a fiery red or a milder green.

Festive and daily fare

Although *papas arrugadas con mojo* are found nowhere else in Spanish territory, much of modern Canary Island cuisine is derived from Spanish cooking. Domingo Navarro's description of a Canarian banquet in the late eighteenth or early nineteenth century does not differ radically from similar celebrations on the mainland. 'By each place appeared four flat dishes and a bowl, with serviette, a spoon, knife and forks, a glass, a wine glass and a bread roll of white flour. A bottle of mellow wine...for each pair of diners and several others of water. A dish of olives and another of anchovies by each place setting and various salad bowls containing beans, lettuce and cucumber. After the soup, a substantial broth of fine noodles, came the traditional stew of large pieces of beef and meat, two chickens, sausages and the

47. Pruned vines, Lanzarote. Each vine is protected by a low wall of lava blocks. The soil here is covered with water-retentive black *picón* (volcanic ash) to keep the plants from drying out.

usual vegetables — potatoes, sweet potatoes, cabbage, beans and tender maize cobs, calabashes, onions and pears.' This 'succulent hors d'oeuvres', as Navarro calls it, is a particularly rich *caldo*. Nowadays a *potaje*, which usually has *berros* (a large-leafed watercress) as its main ingredient, would be served. Then came the 'faggots, a Genoese-style stir-fry and roast leg of pork, kidneys in tomatoes, eels, pigeons, and a meat stew'. When these dishes had been disposed of, the main course appeared: 'a ham between two roast turkeys, and at each end of the table a sphere of stuffed meat and a quarter of roast lamb surrounded by roast potatoes in a sauce'. This was followed in its turn by an equally substantial array of desserts, including a decorated 'cake' of solid marzipan, and liqueurs.

In peasant houses the daily fare was very different. At the end of the nineteenth century Grau-Bassas, probably the first modern writer to record Canarian folk culture, described a Canary Island peasant family's meal thus: 'The "table" was laid on a palm mat on the floor, such is the poverty of the cave-house. On the mat is placed a white cloth, and the whole family sits around it; the women with their legs crossed and the men lying outstretched, resting on their left elbows. A cooking pot of doubtful nature is put beside the woman of the house. This pot sits in a small, flat-bottomed basket. If broth is to be eaten part of it is scooped out into a metal or wooden vessel and in this the *gofio*, kept in a handy *zurrón*...is mixed with it. Each person takes his spoon and eats from the communal trough. When the meal is of meat or fish, this is put in the same common dish with *mojo* sauce and the potatoes cooked in their skins are emptied out on to the cloth. They also mix part of the potatoes, especially those which have split in the cooking, ... with *gofio*.'

The food was washed down with water. Some Canarian spring waters were regarded as medicinal spa waters by tourists early in the twentieth century, though sadly the excessive demands made by modern mass tourism on the islands' ground waters have dried out some of these springs.

Wine

Canary Island wines enjoyed considerable prestige in Europe from as early as the sixteenth century: *malvasía* (malmsey) was well known in Tudor England and referred to by Shakespeare. Malmseys are still produced on Lanzarote; the vines are grown behind stone wind-breaks placed around slight depressions in the

48. A reconstructed wine-press (*lagar*) at the 1989 La Palma Craft Fair, Mazo, La Palma. The carved timber screw in the foreground operates the press.

49. A *queso tierno* (a mild, moist cheese of goat's and sheep's milk) from Valsequillo, Gran Canaria. The pattern of the wooden *quesera* is preserved on the flat surfaces of the cheese, and the imprint left by the basketry mould is clearly seen on the sides.

volcanic ash soils. Drunk on Lanzarote, the local wines complement the harsh and barren landscape; elsewhere they seem to retain the asperity of the pumice in which they are grown. Small *bodegas* (wineries) exist on all the islands, making and selling their own products. A few still possess a *lagar* (wine-press) of traditional type, but all of these wooden presses, operated by an enormous screw, are now derelict.

Fish

The seas around the Canary Islands are rich in fish and both fish and shellfish have always been an important element in the Canarian diet. *Sancocho*, a stew of salted sea bass, potatoes, sweet potato and other vegetables, is served with *mojo* sauce. (This often appears unappetisingly greasy to foreign visitors.)

The various grilled fish (such as *vieja* or *sama*) are particularly tasty, as are whole sardines fried in a light batter. Limpets cooked in a griddle pan are also considered a delicacy.

Cheese

Apart from fish, another important source of protein, both before the European conquest and today, is cheese: cheesemaking is one agricultural craft that has remained virtually unchanged since pre-conquest times. Using the *quesera* (see chapter 5) as a base, the cheese is formed within a basketry container; on the softer cheeses the basketwork impressions show clearly on the sides of the finished cheese. The cheeses are made of goat's, sheep's or cow's milk, or any two of these together, though goat's and sheep's milk are the commonest ingredients of Canarian cheeses.

Cheeses are often made in their spare time by village housewives, who then sell any surplus to their neighbours. This

50. Making cheese in Guía, Gran Canaria, during the local (and modern) Cheese Festival. The cheese in its basketry mould sits on a *quesera* in front of the seated woman.

cottage industry is found on all the islands of the archipelago, although much cheese is now produced in commercial dairies. Each island, and often each village, has its own cheese: in Gran Canaria, the town of Guía is famous for its excellent *queso flor* and El Hierro for its cheeses cured in cellars or caves, while Fuerteventuran cheese (*queso majorero*) is also of high quality.

Unique cultural heritage

The variety of the islands' cheeses reflects the diversity of the islands themselves, their crafts and traditions. Rooted in a North African, Berber past, Canarian customs have adopted, and adapted to, Spanish, South American and North European influences to produce a unique cultural heritage. That heritage has only recently begun to succumb, after surviving Francoist proscription, to the pressures of commercial agriculture and mass tourism.

9
Places to visit

Gran Canaria

Museo Canario, Calle Dr Chil 25, 35001 Las Palmas. Thoroughly modernised in 1986, this museum possesses the finest collection of pre-conquest Canarian material in the world. Nearby is the cathedral with its *Diocesan Museum*, behind which is the *Casa de Colón* (Columbus's House), a late fifteenth-century patio house which houses a collection of Columbus-period relics and from time to time holds temporary exhibitions of crafts. In this part of Las Palmas, the Vegueta, and in the Calle Peregrina in nearby Triana, there are a number of shops selling authentic Canarian craft pottery, basketry and knives.

Cho' Zacarias, San Mateo. A Canarian restaurant and craft museum housed in a rambling group of traditional buildings.

Museo de la Fortaleza, Santa Lucía. A Canarian restaurant and museum containing archaeological and craft objects.

Museo de Piedras (*Stone Museum*), Ingenio. A restaurant where Canarian openwork is made on the premises.

Tenerife

Museo Arqueológico, second floor, Cabildo Insular, Calle Bravo Murillo, Santa Cruz. Pre-Hispanic and some ethnographic material, including a hand-operated mill from Gomera.

The transhumance use of the Teide area is displayed in the *National Park Visitor Centre* at El Portillo.

The small towns along the north coast from the university town of La Laguna to Icod, excluding the tourist resort of Puerto de la Cruz, have most to offer.

Lanzarote

There is a small archaeological museum in the *Castillo de San Gabriel*, Arrecife. The villages of Teguise and Haría are markets for pottery and basketry.

Fuerteventura

In Betancuria there is a small archaeological and ethnographic museum. In the restaurant opposite demonstrations of mixing *gofio* in a *zurrón* are provided for tourists. Antigua is the home of the *Mafasca* craft co-operative.

La Palma, El Hierro and Gomera

The least developed of the Canaries, the three western islands preserve much of their traditional life-styles. La Palma still produces hand-rolled cigars and hand-spun silks.

10
Further reading

Despite a century of close commercial links between Britain and the Canary Islands, remarkably little about the islands' culture has been published in English. Even the growth of tourism since the 1960s has not improved the situation as tourist guidebooks invariably concentrate on sun, sand and sea, and little else.

From the travel literature perhaps the most authoritative books, though now outdated, are:

Mercer, J. *Canary Islands: Fuerteventura*. David and Charles, 1973.

Myhill, H. *The Canary Islands*. Faber, 1972.

The most informative modern book in English on the history and culture of the islands is:

Mercer, J. *The Canary Islanders: Their Prehistory, Conquest and Survival*. Rex Collings, 1980.

For the early colonial period in particular see:

Fernández Armesto, F. *The Canary Islands after the Conquest: the Making of a Colonial Society in the Early Sixteenth Century*. Clarendon, 1982.

There is nothing in English on surviving crafts and traditions. The most useful review is:

Alonso, E. *Folklore Canario*. Edirca, Las Palmas de Gran Canaria, 1985. Deals mainly with festivals, music and sports; contains a list of selected reading and is illustrated in colour.

Index

Page numbers in italic refer to illustrations.